Trauma Care for the Worst Case Scenario

2nd Edition

Gunner Morgan

Trauma Care for the Worst Case Scenario, 2nd Edition

Table of Contents

Introduction

We live in a world where bad things happen to good people. Oftentimes such events happen with little or no warning. From acts of violence to accidents our lives can be forever changed in the blink of an eye. Your ability to assess and treat traumatic injuries in a timely manner may be the difference between life and death or loss of a limb. As a society we have become overly reliant on first responders to help us and provide transport to treatment facilities such as a Level 1 trauma hospital. We assume that we can always call 9-1-1 and help is on the way. This may work the majority of the time but what if there is a major incident and help is not on the way or the phone lines are so tied up that your call won't go through or phone service is completely down. During the events of September 11, 2001 and the Boston Marathon bombing phone service was overwhelmed and not reliable. Or, you may be on a remote trip where there is no cellular phone service and help is miles away. It is imperative that you receive some medical training to deal with situations where help is not coming or is significantly delayed. Without such training you will feel completely helpless or even responsible for not being able to provide help when a loved one, friend, or complete stranger is looking to you for help. That is a terrible feeling to have and it is one that you do not need to experience. There are so many types of medical training classes available these days that there literally is no excuse not to have some training.

Trauma from what?

Trauma can be a result of:

- Active Shooter
- Vehicle Accident
- Stabbing
- Fight
- Fall

- Act of Terrorism
- Natural Disaster
- Structural Failure
- Civil Unrest / Mob
- Violent Protests

The focus of this book is going to be dealing with <u>traumatic injuries and not medical conditions</u> such as a heart attack, stroke, diabetes, anaphylaxis due to bites or stings, or other conditions. While medical conditions are important to understand and have <u>the ability to treat they will not be our priority with this book.</u>

Instead we are going to look at treatment of severe life-threatening bleeding and treatment of an open chest wound. Because some injuries are the result of violent encounters, tactical priorities will also be addressed using a military model applied to civilians.

According to the CDC, Injury is the Leading Cause of Death among Persons Ages 1-44[i]

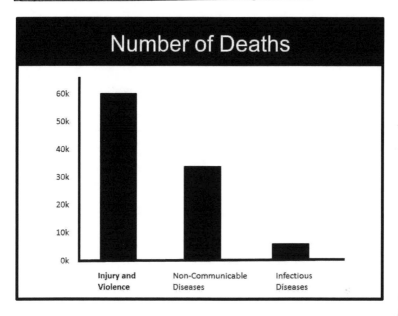

According to the National Trauma Institute[ii]:

The Facts About Trauma in the U.S.

- Trauma is the **#1** cause of death for Americans between 1 and 44 years old.

- Trauma is the **#3** cause of death overall.

- Each year, trauma accounts for 41 million ER visits and 2 million hospital admissions.

- Trauma injury accounts for 30% of all life years lost.

- The economic burden of trauma is more than $406 billion annually.

- Each year, more than 180,000 people lose their lives to trauma.

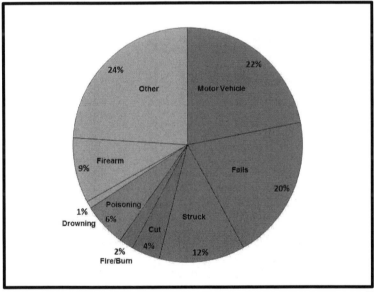

iii

Clearly, trauma is a major factor that has significant impact on society in terms of lost lives, injuries, and costs. Trauma is not an issue that is limited to the United States. Injuries and violence are a major public health issue worldwide and account for nearly 1 out of every 10 deaths every year.[iv]

- Globally, more than nine people die every minute from injuries or violence—that's 5.8 million people of all ages and economic groups who die each year from both unintentional and violence related injuries!

- The three leading causes of injury and violence-related deaths are road traffic *global* incidents (1.3 million), suicides (844,000), and homicides (600,000).

- In addition, millions of people seek medical treatment due to injuries and violence.

- Violence can result in serious injuries and even death, but may also lead to other significant mental and physical health consequences such as depression and anxiety, pregnancy complications, and even chronic diseases such as diabetes and heart disease.

- Violence also erodes the sense of safety and security so essential to the well-being of families and communities.

This book is targeted for law enforcement officers, military personnel, correctional officers, detention officers, probation & parole officers, court security officers, preppers, responsible firearms owners and others who want to know what medical gear to carry for treating the worst case scenario.

When *"time is of the essence"* you must be prepared and ready to respond.

Options for Medical Training

Many organizations and schools offer basic through advanced medical training. Oftentimes these training classes are taught at times that are convenient for even the busiest schedule. You can take classes during the evening and on weekends. You can even take some basic classes online from the comfort of your home. While such classes typically do not "certify" you in the training you will still receive valuable knowledge. If you work in law enforcement or the military then training opportunities will be provided that are free. Some corporations that you may work for offer free basic first aid and CPR classes. Take advantage of these opportunities. Regardless of where you obtain your medical training it is imperative that you train and practice your skills on a regular basis and under stressful condition. Medical training much like self-defense and firearms skills are perishable meaning that you will lose the skill if you do not practice on a regular basis. You want to be confident enough in your ability that you could treat a person any time and any place at a moment's notice oftentimes under less than ideal circumstances. Remember, most emergencies happen at the blink of an eye and you may not get advance notice of an impending situation. Your ability to perform well is directly correlated to your knowledge, skills, abilities, and experience. Another option is to volunteer with a local fire department or do ride-alongs to get some valuable hands on experience.

<u>Training options include:</u>

> - Basic First Aid along with CPR, CCR, & AED
>
> - Community Emergency Response Team (CERT)
>
> - Wilderness First Aid
>
> - Emergency Medical Technician (EMT)
>
> - Paramedic
>
> -Trauma First Responder[v]
>
> - Specialty classes to enhance skills
>
> - Military Training –
>
> > ▪ Combat Lifesaver (CLS)
> >
> > ▪ Combat Medic
>
> - Law Enforcement Training –
>
> > ▪ Self-Aid, Buddy Aid (SABA)

- Basic Tactical Casualty Care (BTCC)

- Tactical EMS (TEMS)

Basic first aid classes are often free or very inexpensive and do not require a lot of time. Every CERT class that I am aware of is free through your local fire department. Emergency Medical Technician classes can be completed in as little as 10 weeks or one semester at a community college. EMT is the minimum level of training that I recommend as it will provide you with a solid foundation of basic emergency care. Paramedic training is much more comprehensive and requires a commitment to the training. Some agencies will pay for your training as well. There are a lot of options available that will greatly enhance your ability to help those in need.

There are also specialty classes that can incorporate specific medical training on topics such as extrication, search and rescue, technical rescue, swift water rescue, etc. Before you consider such classes it is best to master the basics, Take the necessary time to learn the basics so that you can use them under less than ideal circumstances when under stress. You must also have the ability to treat yourself if seriously injured. This will require that you develop a mindset that you will never give up. Can you imagine having to put a tourniquet on your upper arm due to an amputation in a motor vehicle accident or from an improvised explosive device (IED)? Or maybe you need to apply a tourniquet to your wife who was accidently shot in the femoral artery. You need the ability to block out the emotions of the situation and take care of priorities. This requires realistic training.

Having the skill to perform self-aid or buddy-aid is critical. You cannot assume, even when working in an urban environment, that medical care will be able to reach your location to provide aid. In an active shooter incident law enforcement officers will move past you to hunt down the shooter. Fire department and medical personnel, who have the ability to provide lifesaving care, will be required to stage some distance away from the scene. You may be in a situation where you are being held down by gunfire which prohibits first responders from getting to you. Or, you may be the subject of a hostage/barricaded situation where you have sustained potentially life threatening injuries. Again, never assume that first responders will be capable of helping you. It is incumbent upon you to be able to provide self-aid or buddy-aid until a higher level of care will be able to provide medical assistance or until you can reach a hospital.

> *Remember, it is possible that in some situations no one is coming to your aid. You will be reliant on the skills and medical equipment that you have available.*

Disclaimer

This book is designed to expose you to medical concepts.

While some of the information is what you obtain in basic

first aid training, other components may be considered

beyond first aid. You are highly encouraged to seek

further training and skill development.

Do NOT perform care above your level of training.

It cannot be stressed enough that you should never provide medical care above your level of training otherwise you may be opening yourself up to liability and potentially criminal charges.

In life or death situations you may have to make serious decisions in a timely manner. It is incumbent upon you to be prepared for the potential consequences of your decisions. Quality training can help you know which decisions are correct and what type of medical care to provide. The bottom line is that you need to receive training from a credible source.

Prevention

Before we move on to the main content of this book let's talk a little about prevention. The ultimate goal is that you never have to use your medical training. While this is the goal it may also be considered wishful thinking based on the previously listed statistics. Realistically, there are many things that you can do to avoid traumatic injury.

Following are suggestions that I recommend:

- If you are engaging in a dangerous event wear appropriate protection such as a helmet and pads.

- Receive proper training from an experienced expert in the field of activity that you are going to participate.

- If you ride a motorcycle wear a helmet. I used to work as an emergency medical technician and I never responded to a motorcycle accident with minor injuries. All of them resulted in severe facial and head injuries. Some of the injuries resulted in death while others suffered lifelong injury such as paralysis, brain damage, and/or significant disfigurement. These injuries could have been prevented or minimized with a helmet.

- When riding a bicycle, skateboard or other similar device always wear a helmet and protective gear.

- Do not enter a vehicle with an impaired driver whether from drugs, alcohol, or certain prescription medication.

- Do not text and drive.

- Do not engage in activities while driving that distract you from safely operating the vehicle.

- Always wear a seatbelt and make sure that it is properly applied. Too many people keep their seatbelt too loose which limits the amount of protection it can provide.

- When around firearms always follow appropriate safety procedures and gun safety rules.

- Avoid dangerous locations when possible.

- When possible don't interject yourself into a potentially dangerous situation.

- Maintain situational awareness at all times

when you are out of the safety and comfort of your home. Know who is around you, where exits are located, and be aware of what is occurring.

- Avoid illegal drug use. You would be amazed at the stupid things people do while under the influence of drugs.

- Avoid alcohol in excess. Again, like drugs, people tend to do stupid things and place themselves in dangerous situations when under the influence of alcohol.

- Never drive under the influence of alcohol, drugs, and certain prescription medications.

- Use your brain and **think before you act**. There are so many videos on the internet of people doing dangerous stunts that result in severe injury and death.

You cannot avoid all bad things from happening but take some responsibility for the things that you can avoid. People who engage in unsafe activities should expect something to eventually go wrong especially if you fail to take the activity seriously, do not follow safety procedures and choose not to use utilize safety equipment.

Patient Assessment

The ability to perform an accurate patient assessment is critical so that you do not miss any injuries that must take priority over other injuries. Yet, it is important to keep in mind that you will more than likely not have all the medical equipment that you need such as a blood pressure cuff. But, you should have basic medical supplies to treat traumatic injuries. In such cases you may not be able to obtain necessary vital signs such as blood pressure. Also, without a watch it is difficult to obtain an *accurate* assessment of the patient's heart rate and respirations. Sometimes you just have to make do with what you have. Keep in mind that when talking about trauma care for the **worst case scenario** it is important to point out that you are not a first responder who is tasked with providing care. The assumption made with this book is that you are prepared to take care of yourself, family, and friends. If you choose you can take care of others but your priority is yourself, family, and friends. Every once in a while I run into an individual who literally is carrying a backpack full of medical supplies. They carry this pack with them everywhere just waiting for the chance to treat someone. This is what is called a *"trauma junkie."* If you feel the need to carry such a kit then become an EMT or paramedic and become a professional medical provider.

Before the patient assessment even begins it is important to take note of the following:

- Your safety is the number one priority

- Personal Protection – Use of gloves, goggles, etc. **Always use gloves when coming into contact with bodily fluids**

- Scene Safety – Remove patient from immediate danger if possible and without putting yourself at risk

- Mechanism of Injury (MOI) – What caused the injury such as car accident, fall, gunshot wound, assault, etc.

- If you drive upon an accident be sure to park your vehicle in a safe location so that you are not a hazard to yourself or others.

- Maintain situational awareness as you may not fully appreciate the situation that you find yourself entering. You may unintentionally find yourself in the middle of a violent situation. Just because you are there "to help" does not mean that you will not become a victim.

Assessment of the Trauma Patient

A. Major Components of the Patient Assessment

1. Standard precautions

2. Scene size-up

3. General impression

4. Mechanism of injury

5. Primary assessment

6. Baseline vital signs

7. History

8. Secondary assessment

9. Re-assessment

B. Mechanism of Injury (MOI)

1. Significant MOI (including, but not limited to)

a. Multiple body systems injured

b. Vehicle Crashes with intrusion

c. Falls from heights

d. Pedestrian vs. vehicle collision

e. Motorcycle crashes

f. Death of a vehicle occupant in the same vehicle

2. Non-significant MOI (including, but not limited to)

   a. Isolated trauma to a body part

   b. Falls without loss of consciousness

3. Pediatric considerations

   a. Falls - **>10** feet without loss of consciousness

   b. Falls - **<10** feet with loss of consciousness

   c. Bicycle collision

   d. Medium - to high-speed vehicle collision (>25 mph)

4. Re-evaluating the MOI

5. Special Considerations

   a. Spinal precautions must be initiated soon as practical based on the MOI

   b. When practical, roll the supine *(patient who is on their back)* patient on their side to allow for an appropriate assessment of the posterior body

c. Consider the need for advanced life support (ALS) backup for all patients who have sustained a significant MOI (Remember, ALS may not be coming to help)

Patient Assessment:

During your assessment of the patient your goal is to identify and treat life-threatening problems concentrating on:

- Level of Consciousness (LOC)

- Cervical Spine (CS) Stabilization

- Airway

- Breathing

- Circulation and Bleeding

- General Impression of the Patient – How does the patient look? It is a male or female, age, type of injury, number of injuries, number of patients, etc.

- Determine Level of Consciousness – AVPU

Alert	Patient is awake
Verbal	Responds to verbal stimulation
Pain	Responds to painful stimulation
Unresponsive	Patient does not respond

- Chief Complaint – If possible, ask what is wrong.

    Remember, if a patient is able to talk then they are moving some air which is a positive sign. If the person becomes unable to speak that may be an indication of an airway problem.

- Airway – Does the patient have an open and clear airway?

    A. <u>Signs of Adequate Airway</u>

    1. Airway is open, can hear or feel air move in and out

    2. Patient is speaking in full sentences

    3. Sound of the voice is normal

B. <u>Signs of Inadequate Airway</u>

   1. Unusual sounds are heard with breathing such as:

      a. Stridor - a harsh, grating, or creaking sound

      b. Snoring

   2. Awake patient is unable to speak or sounds hoarse

   3. No air movement (known as apnea)

   4. Airway obstruction

      a. Tongue

      b. Food

      c. Vomit

      d. Blood

      e. Teeth

      f. Foreign body

C. Swelling Due to Trauma or Infection

D. Airway Status

1. <u>Unresponsive patient</u>

   a. Medical patients

      i. Open and maintain the airway with head-tilt, chin-lift technique

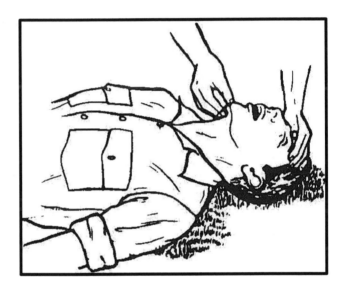

   b. Trauma patients

      i. Open and maintain the airway with modified jaw thrust technique while maintaining manual cervical stabilization

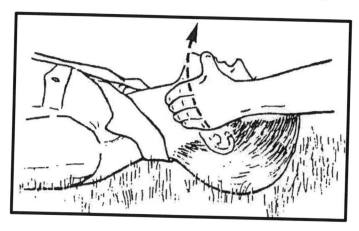

2. <u>Responsive patient</u>

    a. If the patient speaks, the airway is functional but may still be at risk -- foreign body or substances in the mouth may impair the airway and must be removed

        i. Finger sweep (solid objects)

        ii. Suction (liquids)

    b. If the upper airway becomes narrowed, inspiration may produce a high-pitched whistling sound known as stridor

        i. Foreign body

        ii. Swelling

iii. Trauma

c. Airway patency (open airway) must be continually reassessed

▪ Breathing – Is breathing adequate? Is the patient struggling to breath, snoring, gurgling, wheezing, etc.

Respiration (Ventilation) Rates:

<12	Slow
12-20	Normal
21-30	Fast
>30	Abnormally Fast

1. Signs of adequate ventilation

   a. Respiratory rate is normal
   b. Breath sounds are clear on both sides of the chest (chances are you will not have access to a stethoscope to check breath sounds)
      i. Anterior (front)
      ii. Posterior (back)

2. <u>Signs of inadequate ventilation</u>

    a. Abnormal breathing

        i. Retractions

        ii. Nasal flaring

        iii. Abdominal breathing

        iv. Diaphoresis (perspiration)

    b. Abnormal breath sounds

        i. Stridor

        ii. Wheezing

        iii. Crackles

        iv. Silent chest

        v. Breath sounds are unequal

            a) Trauma

            b) Infection

            c) Pneumothorax

    c. Chest wall movement or damage

    d. Irregular respiratory pattern

3. Breathing Status

1. <u>Patient responsive</u>

   a. Breathing is adequate

   (rate and quality)

   b. Breathing is too fast

   (**>24** breaths per minute)

   c. Breathing is too slow

   (**<8** breaths per minute)

   d. Breathing absent (choking)

2. <u>Patient unresponsive</u>

   a. Breathing is adequate (rate

   and quality)

   b. Breathing is inadequate

   c. Breathing is absent

- Circulation – Is circulation adequate?

   Control all severe hemorrhage

Heart Rate:

<60	Slow
60-100	Normal
>100	Fast

A. Circulatory Status

    1. Radial pulse present (rate and quality)

        a. Normal rate

        b. Fast

        c. Slow

        d. Irregular rate

    2. Radial pulse absent

    3. Assess if major bleeding is present

    4. Perfusion status

        a. Skin color

        b. Skin temperature

        c. Skin moisture

        d. Capillary refill

- Life Threatening Injury

  4. Assess patient and determine if the patient has a life-threatening condition

     a. Unstable – If a life threatening condition is found, treat immediately

     b. Stable – Assess nature of illness or mechanism of injury

Rapid Trauma Assessment

Pre-hospital professionals such as EMTs and paramedics use what is called a Rapid Trauma Assessment when dealing with traumatic injuries. While you would not necessarily use the exact same process I have modified this assessment for non-professionals. This assessment is performed on patients with significant mechanism of injury (MOI) to determine potential life threatening injuries. With the conscious patient, symptoms should be sought before and during the Rapid Trauma assessment. You will estimate the severity of the injuries, re-consider your transport options, when possible obtain a higher level of care from medical professionals, rapidly assess the patient from head to toe using **DCAP-BTLS**, obtain a baseline set of vital signs if possible, and perform a **SAMPLE** history. While you may not be able to obtain a blood pressure you should wear a watch to obtain an accurate pulse and respirations.

DCAP-BTLS is a mnemonic in which each area of the body is evaluated for:

- **D**eformities

- **C**ontusions

- **A**brasions

- **P**unctures/Penetrations

- **B**urns

- **T**enderness

- **L**acerations

- **S**welling

The goal with this process is so that you do not miss any injuries that require immediate treatment and so that you are performing a quick, yet thorough, patient examination. It is important to always keep in mind that when dealing with serious injuries time is of the essence and the quicker that you are able to provide necessary care the better chance your patient has for survival.

Areas to check are the:

- Head

- Neck

- Chest

- Abdomen

- Pelvic region

- Extremities

Do not forget to check both the front and back of the patient.

<u>Head</u>

- Check hair for soft tissue injuries

- Check pupils looking for size reactions to light, equality in size

- Carefully feel (palpate) the bones of the face and skull to check for any irregularities such as depressions, fractures, deviations, etc.

Neck

- Conduct a visual examination of the neck region looking for any sign of injury to include lacerations, bruising, abrasions, and deformities. Carefully check for tenderness of the cervical spine which may indicate a neck injury. Ensure that the cervical spine remains in a neutral and in-line position to avoid potential further damage if there is a cervical injury to the spine.

Chest

- The chest (thorax) is strong, flexible, and resilient and can withstand a lot of trauma. When examining the chest you are looking for deformities, contusions, abrasions, and unequal movement of the chest wall. Without the use of a stethoscope it will be difficult to evaluate air movement within the lungs.

Abdomen

- Visually examine the abdomen for abrasions, contusions, and lacerations. Palpitate the abdomen for tenderness, masses, and rigidity. The concern with abdominal injury is damage to organs and internal bleeding.

Pelvis

- Visually examine the pelvis for abrasions, contusions, lacerations, fractures and distension. Pelvic distension may be a result from a fracture that causes significant internal bleeding.

Extremities

- Visually examine each bone and joint for deformity, bruising, and lacerations. Palpitate for pain, tenderness, and unusual movement indicating a potential fracture. All suspected fractures should be immobilized to prevent further injury. Check distal pulse both before and after splinting.

<u>Back</u>

- Remember to check the back for potential injury. When indicated be sure to take cervical spine (C-spine) precautions.

SAMPLE is a mnemonic for the history of a patient's condition to determine:

- **S**igns & **S**ymptoms

    <u>Signs</u> are what you observe.

    <u>Symptoms</u> are what the patient

    tells you.

- **A**llergies

- **M**edications

- **P**ertinent Past History

- **L**ast Oral Intake (Food and liquids)

- **E**vents leading up to illness/injury

SAMPLE in more detail:

- Symptoms – What is the patients complaint? i.e. pain, numbness, nausea, difficulty breathing, lightheaded, dizzy, etc.

- Allergies – Is the patient allergic to any medications?

- Medications – What medications, both prescription and non-prescription, is the patient taking?

- Pertinent Past History – Significant medical problems that required the patient to receive medical care to include prior surgical procedures?

- Last Oral Intake – When was the patients last meal? Trauma often requires surgery and recent food intake can increase the risk of aspiration (chocking.)

- Events leading up to illness/injury – Did the event have a correlation to the injury?

Depending on your situation and location one of the aspects that you will need to consider is how and where you are going to transport the patient for more advanced medical care or if this even a possibility. The worst case scenario might mean a breakdown of society where services are unavailable, you might be in an area where you cannot reach emergency services, or you are the patient are trapped and unable to move. Never assume someone else is coming to your aid. This is the worst case scenario.

Pathophysiology of the Trauma Patient

Traumatic injuries can be the result of blunt force trauma or penetrating trauma. An example of blunt force trauma is being in a vehicular accident and your chest hits the steering wheel. Another example is getting hit in the chest and abdomen with a baseball bat during an assault. Examples of penetrating trauma would be a gunshot wound or getting stabbed with a sharp instrument.

A. Blunt Trauma - A traumatic injury effected by a blunt object or force, in which the skin was not penetrated; usually results from assaults, abuse, accidents or resuscitative measures.[vi]

1. Non-bleeding (*Just because you do not see bleeding does not mean that the injury is not serious. Internal bleeding can be very serious and result to death.*)

2. Multiple forces and conditions can cause blunt trauma

B. Penetrating Trauma – A wound that breaks the skin and enters into a body area, organ, or cavity.[vii]

Penetrating trauma can be considered high, medium, and low velocity.

Patient Assessment/Management - Trauma

Scene Size Up
Determine the scene is safe
Determine mechanism of injury (MOI)
Determine number of patients
Obtain assistance if possible
Considers stabilization of the spine
Primary Survey / Resuscitation
Obtain general impression of patient
Determine Responsiveness / Level of Consciousness - AVPU
Determine Chief Complaint/Life Threatening Injuries

Airway:
   _ Open Airway
   _ Assess Airway
   _ Insert adjunct as indicated

Breathing:
   _ Assess adequate ventilation
   _ Manage injury(s) which compromise breathing

Circulation:
   _ Check pulse
   _ Assess skin (color, temperature)
   _ Control severe hemorrhage
   _ Treat for shock

Secondary Assessment
Head: _ Assess _ Inspect _ Palpate Face, scalp, eyes, ears
Neck: _ Assess _ Inspect _ Palpate Trachea, jugular, cervical
Chest: _ Inspect _ Palpate _ Auscultate
Abdomen/Pelvis: _ Assess _ Inspect _ Palpate
Extremities: _ Assess _ Inspect _ Palpate
Posterior: _ Inspect _ Palpate
Vital Signs: Blood Pressure, Pulse, Respirations   You may not have access to a blood pressure cuff
Reassessment: Every 15 minutes

It is important to remember that as a lay person you probably will not have access to all the equipment that will aid in a proper assessment and treatment. This can include a blood pressure cuff, cervical spine immobilization, splints, oxygen, etc. Do not let this reality prevent you from providing care that you can provide to the patient. Do the best with what you have and adapt to the situation.

Trauma Care

Trauma and medical care continues to improve
and is constantly changing to keep up with
advancements in medical research, practice, and
experience. Many medical improvements, especially
relating to trauma, come directly from the military and
are then assimilated into civilian medical care. The
wars in Iraq and Afghanistan have provided a lot of
new information relating to the treatment of traumatic
injuries. Keep in mind that this book is about dealing
with trauma and not medical conditions.

> **The provided information is NOT a**
>
> **substitute for receiving hands on training**
>
> **from a qualified medical provider.**

You must have the ability to perform self-aid when
alone and buddy-aid when with another person. Even
when help may be enroute to your location some
injuries can be so severe that you must perform
assistance either to yourself or another person to
prevent death prior to help arriving. Even if help is
going to arrive in approximately 5 minutes you can
bleed to death in that time from a severe injury.

Based in data from the military preventable causes of combat death include[viii]:

61%   Hemorrhage from Extremity Wounds

33%   Tension Pneumothorax

6%   Airway Obstruction

Considering that 61% of preventable deaths are from ***extremity wound hemorrhaging*** it shows that a main priority is to control severe bleeding effectively and early especially when help may be delayed. <u>This is a skill that you must have the ability to perform.</u>

Trauma Care

*"**90%** of combat deaths occur on the battlefield before the casualty ever reaches a medical treatment facility."*

- Col. Ron Bellamy

"The hemorrhage that takes place when a main artery is divided is usually so rapid and so copious that the wounded man dies before help can reach him."

- Col. H.M. Gray, 1919

Blood

- Adult body:

  - Contains approximately 5 to 6 liters of blood

  - Loss of 1 pint of blood without harmful effects

  - Loss of 2 pints may cause shock

External Bleeding

Significant blood loss

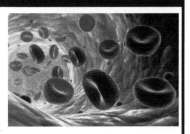

- 1 liter - Adult

- 1/2 liter - Child

- 100 to 200 ml - Infant

Result may be HYPOVOLEMIC shock

A ***tension pneumothorax*** is life threatening condition where air progressively builds up in the chest cavity typically due to a lung laceration such as from a gunshot wound or from being stabbed in the chest. Air pressure collapses the lung and pushes it on the heart. The heart becomes compressed and is not able to pump blood well which can lead to death if not treated. The treatment consists of a needle thoracotomy, also known as a needle decompression, which can be done in the field but is above the skill level of most individuals.

A tension pneumothorax can be minimized or prevented by treating an open "sucking" chest wound with the use of an occlusive dressing. This is a skill that you can apply. An open chest wound can be caused by the chest wall being penetrated by a bullet, knife, or other object. When a person with an open chest wound breathes, air goes in and out of the wound and may cause a "sucking" sound. Due to the distinct sound an open chest wound is often called a "sucking chest wound."

> *The ability to rapidly and effectively treat severe bleeding from an extremity wound and an open chest wound can increase survival rates by a significant amount.*

Considering this information, it is important that you carry a first aid kit so that they have the ability to treat such wounds. Oftentimes such a first aid kit is referred to as an Individual First Aid Kit (IFAK). Contents of an IFAK will be discussed later.

The use of tourniquets has been controversial in civilian pre-hospital care settings but has been the recommended management for all life threatening hemorrhage by the military. The benefits of tourniquet use over other methods include:

- In a situation where you have an active threat that is attempting to kill you it will be difficult to apply direct pressure and compression especially if you are trying to move to a safer location or behind cover. Remember, you are still being engaged from an active threat.

- Tourniquets can be applied by yourself (self-aid) thereby reducing the chance of someone else getting injured as they attempt to get to your location.

- There are few complications with tourniquet use relating to ischemic (lack of blood supply) damage especially if in place for less than two hours.

- In Iraq and Afghanistan tourniquets have

proven their effectiveness in saving many lives.

Tactical Combat Casualty Care (TCCC)

The military uses a concept called <u>Tactical Combat Casualty Care</u> (TCCC) which defines medical and combat priorities on the battlefield. Utilizing TCCC principles emphasizes extremity hemorrhage control over airway management when there is still an active threat which is called <u>Care Under Fire</u>. Tourniquet application to control life threatening extremity hemorrhage is the only procedure used while there is an active threat. Your priorities in a Care Under Fire incident are:

- Stopping the threat from firing at you which is most effectively accomplished if you are armed with a firearm

- Moving to a position of safety behind appropriate cover

- Treating severe life-threatening bleeding

In a Care Under Fire incident you are in the "*hot zone*" and must maintain your situational awareness to know where the threat is at all times. Do what you can to stop the threat from injuring you which is accomplished much more easily if you are armed. If you are not armed you are at a significant disadvantage when faced with an armed assailant because you are limited in your response options. Regardless of whether you are armed or not it is important to scan the environment for cover. Scanning will not only provide you with situational awareness it will also aid in avoiding tunnel vision (loss of peripheral vision) so that you do not get overly focused or "missile locked" on obtaining cover to the point that you lose sight of the threat. In the absence of cover your best tactic is to keep moving as it is much more difficult to hit a dynamic moving target as opposed to a static target.

Contrary to popular misconceptions people who receive non-lethal penetrating wounds are often not incapacitated and can continue to fight and engage threats. If you are injured while under fire you should attempt to remain engaged, take cover, provide self-aid to control severe hemorrhage and re-engage to stop the threat. You cannot stop fighting when there is an active threat that is attempting to kill you. Doing so will almost guarantee your death which is an unacceptable outcome. If you are injured to the point that you cannot move you may need to "play dead" and possibly the threat will move on. Playing dead may be your last option in the absence of cover and without the ability to move. When safe to do so you must address severe bleeding.

The following illustrates a common saying often used in TCCC:

> *Good medicine can sometimes be bad tactics;*
>
> *Bad tactics can get everyone killed.*
>
> *Doing the right thing at the right time is critical.*
>
> *Doing the right thing at the wrong time can get you killed.*

Your ability to provide pre-hospital care may be the most important factor in determining your survival or the survival of a loved one. Some incidents may require that you make both medical and tactical decisions very fast especially if a perpetrator is attempting to kill you. There is no "time-out" just because you or a loved receives an injury. The lifesaving tactics discussed in this book will not turn you into a special operations paramedic but will give you the skills to provide time critical treatment. Your goal is to perform self-aid or buddy-aid to keep alive long enough to reach the hospital for more advanced medical care. It is bad enough have a perpetrator shoot at you or attack you with a knife but this experience rapidly progresses from bad to worse if you become injured. In this situation you must maintain the mindset to never give up. Being shot, stabbed, or wounded does not mean that you are helpless, out of the fight, or dead.

Do not lie down and die. Never give up.

Not all situations will be violent encounters. Yet, if you are engaged in a violent encounter such as an active shooter situation you will require the use of additional tactics especially when there is still an active threat attempting to hurt you. If you are injured in a vehicle accident, fall, natural disaster, or other event these tactics would not apply and you can focus on providing appropriate care to the wounded.

Basic Plan for Tactical Field Care

Tactical Field Care is care rendered by yourself or another once you are no longer in the line of fire and there is **not** an active threat. This is the time when you can conduct an appropriate assessment and more thoroughly treat injuries based upon your skill level and medical gear that you have on your person. Keep in mind that the military has combat medics available to provide aid during combat and some law enforcement agencies have tactical emergency medical services (TEMS) personnel assigned to SWAT units. You will not have this type of medical backup readily available. The medical equipment you have will consist of the first aid kit you carry or whatever you are able to improvise based on your clothing or what is available in the immediate environment. For example, if you do not have a commercially made tourniquet you may have to improvise one from a belt or other item of clothing. Death from exsanguination (severe blood loss) due to an extremity injury is preventable but requires quick, decisive, and effective action to stop the bleeding. It would be a travesty to lose a life because someone bled to death due to a severe extremity wound. Your goal at this stage is to stay alive by treating life-threatening injuries until paramedic units arrive and can transport you and/or your partner to an appropriate medical facility. If you are in a remote area that requires a long travel time by ground ambulance to a hospital first responders should immediately put an air ambulance helicopter on standby. If your injuries are non-life threatening the helicopter can always be cancelled.

Being shot or severely injured can cause your body to have both psychological and physiological responses that can negatively impact your ability to respond to the situation. It is critical that you maintain focus to control these responses so that you can cognitively process what actions to take to keep yourself or loved one alive. This is especially true in a care under fire incident. Remember to breathe and not hold your breath during periods of extreme stress. The last thing you want to do is hold your breath or hyperventilate and then pass out.

Your Role in a Crisis

Remain Calm:

- **Panic is contagious**

- Calm is also contagious

Even though you may be nervous attempt to show that you are in control so that others remain in control.

Do not forget to breathe.

Tactical Field Care

In a Tactical Field Care situation you are no longer under effective hostile fire. You now have the opportunity to perform appropriate care based on your training. ***Keep in mind that the situation can change and you end up back in a Care Under Fire situation.*** Because events can change it is important to maintain situational awareness of your environment.

Following are guidelines from TCCC modified for civilians:

1. If the person you are treating has an altered mental status and is armed with a firearm you

should disarm this person immediately.

An altered mental status can be the result of shock, hypoxia, or brain injury. Individuals with an altered mental status may lose the ability to cognitively process information and become incapable of using proper judgment about threats. This can be a deadly safety hazard. This person should be immediately disarmed and their weapons rendered safe.

2. Airway Management – Airway intervention does not need to be addressed if the person is conscious and breathing well on her own.

   a. Unconscious without airway obstruction:

      - Chin lift or jaw thrust maneuver
      - Nasopharyngeal airway (NPA) - generally well tolerated if consciousness is regained. **Training should be received prior to using a NPA.**
      - Place in recovery position

   b. Casualty with airway obstruction or impending airway obstruction:

- Chin lift or jaw thrust maneuver
- Nasopharyngeal airway
- Allow casualty to assume any position that best protects the airway, to include sitting up
- Place unconscious casualty in recovery position

Utilization of the recovery position helps a semiconscious or unconscious person breathe and permits fluids such as blood, mucous, or vomit to drain from the nose and throat so they are not breathed in. This position should not be used if there is a back or neck injury.

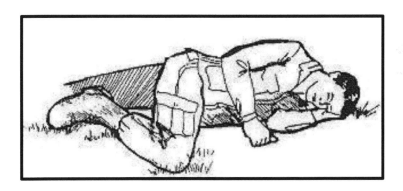

To place someone in the recovery position:

- Roll the person on their side with their arms and upper leg at right angles to the body to support them

- Tuck their upper hand under the side of their head so that their head is resting on the hand

- Open their airway by tilting the head back and lifting the chin

- Monitor their breathing and pulse continuously

For both situations a. and b. listed above you would benefit to receive training on the proper procedure to insert a nasopharyngeal airway which is a tube designed to be inserted into the nasal passageway to secure an open airway. As in a Care Under Fire incident, cervical spine immobilization is generally not required for penetrating injuries and assumes a lower priority than caring for massive hemorrhage or airway obstruction. Cervical spine immobilization should be considered for blunt trauma injuries. If the previous airway management techniques are not effective then the casualty will need treatment from a responder trained with a higher level of care and who can perform an intubation or cricothyroidotomy. Intubation is the placement of a flexible plastic tube into the trachea (windpipe) to maintain an open airway so that the patient can be properly ventilated. A cricothyroidotomy is an emergency surgical procedure in which a hole is cut through a membrane in the patient's neck into the windpipe in order to allow air into the lungs.

Such techniques should never be attempted by untrained individuals.

3. Breathing

   a. Treat all open "sucking" chest wounds (open pneumothorax) with an occlusive dressing and secure it in place.

   b. If a tension pneumothorax develops the person will need a needle chest decompression performed by a paramedic or other medical provider.

      A tension pneumothorax is a life threatening development that is preventable if higher level medical care can get to the person in a timely manner.

4. Bleeding

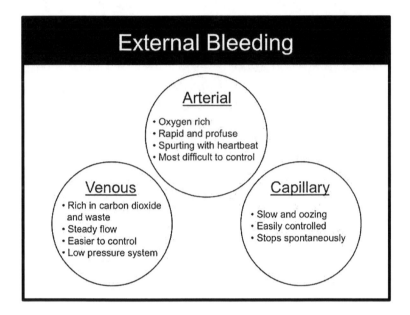

a. Use a tourniquet to control **life threatening hemorrhage** that is amenable to tourniquet application. Do not wait until a patient goes into shock before applying a tourniquet.

b. For hemorrhaging that is not amenable to tourniquet application use a hemostatic agent such as QuikClot Combat Gauze applied with direct pressure for a **minimum of three minutes**. A hemostatic agent is a substance that stops bleeding.

The most common form of hemostatic agent used in a field setting is a dressing.

c. Control other significant bleeding that has not previously been addressed. Remember, blood loss will have a cumulative effect over time which is a factor when help is delayed or not coming at all.

Individual First Aid Kit (IFAK)

Police officers carry a firearm because the need may arise when they will have to use their weapon against a violent offender. They wear body armor just in case they are shot. Everyone should wear seat belts in case they are in an automobile accident. Motorcyclists should wear a helmet every time they ride. Individuals who are training with firearms should use eye and ear protection. We should all take precautions to minimize the risks of bad things that may occur. The point being that bad things can and do happen to good people. And whether they are statistically relevant or not we should take precautions for those times when you just might become the statistic. Carrying an Individual First Aid Kit (IFAK) is one of those items you hope to never have to use but should the need occur the kit can literally save your life, a loved one, or a complete stranger in need.

> **An Individual First Aid Kit (IFAK) is designed to enable you to treat potentially life-threatening traumatic injuries typically associated with gunshot and stab wounds or applicable accidents.**

There are literally dozens of commercially available IFAK's on the market that go by a variety of different names such as: Individual Patrol Officer Kit (IPOK™), Patrol Trauma Pack, Operator IFAK, Basic Life Support Tactical Operator Response Kit (BLS TORK™), Advanced Patrol Officer's Trauma Kit, Patrol Officer's Pocket Trauma Kit, Police Academy Personal Trauma Kit, Tactical First Response Kit, etc. The list goes on and there are many choices to choose from when it comes to your medical kit. Some are good quality while others are lacking. When it comes to your IFAK I cannot stress enough the importance of only carrying quality components. Remember, the kit you carry may save your life one day so don't skimp. Before we discuss IFAK components lets discuss what an IFAK is not.

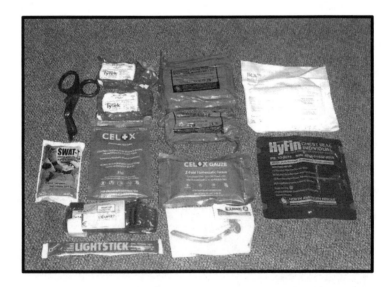

An IFAK is not a "boo-boo" kit designed to treat minor injuries such as cuts, scrapes, blisters, hang nails, sore muscles, or a bloody nose. It is not a place for an assortment of Band-Aids or over the counter medications for pain, allergies, cramps, or headaches. If you are required to take prescription medication throughout the day or as needed those medications would not be included in your IFAK. While the items mentioned do not belong in your IFAK you should have a separate kit to keep such items that will probably be utilized with some regularity. This separate kit can be kept in your work desk, gear bag, or vehicle. ***Your IFAK is reserved specifically for the treatment of life-threatening injuries.***

IFAK Considerations

Choosing an IFAK is an important decision because the time that you need to use the kit will be under the "***worst case scenario***" when someone's life is at risk. You will be nervous, your heart will be pounding, you may breathe faster, your hands may shake, and you might feel like you need to use the restroom. To make matters worse is that '***time is of the essence***' when treating a life-threatening injury such as a severe hemorrhage. Having a quality kit along with the knowledge of how to use each component will give you piece of mind should you ever need to treat yourself or another person.

When choosing an IFAK you can buy one that is a commercially available pre-made IFAK or you can purchase items individually and create a kit to your own specifications. I prefer to create my own IFAK so that I know it will fit my individualized needs.

Following are some considerations when choosing or building an IFAK:

Cost: Basic kits can be very inexpensive but tend to lack needed items. Comprehensive kits will cost more and provide higher quality components.

Quality & Effectiveness	There are many companies that make products that can be placed in an IFAK but not all are equally effective. I recommend only using the highest quality most effective items. For example, there is no sense in having a tourniquet that is small and compact yet will not stop a major hemorrhage.
Size	The more comprehensive your IFAK the larger it will be. Smaller kits tend to lack important components. You will need to find a balance that fits your needs. Sometimes this is easier said than done.
Portability	Whatever IFAK you choose you must commit to carrying it with you at all times as it serves you no good if it is not with you.
Maintenance	Any items that are used will need to be immediately replaced. Some components may have expiration dates.
Training	It is important to train with each component of your kit so that you are completely familiar with

its use and functionality. This may require that you purchase duplicate items so that you can train and become proficient with each component. Also, some items such as a Nasopharyngeal Airway (NPA) may require that you attend formal training or certification in its use.

As with many things in life you can easily come up with a laundry list of excuses not to carry an IFAK. Excuses such as: It is too big, too cumbersome, I will never need it, no one else carries one, it is too expensive, I will wait for paramedics, I hate the sight of blood, etc. Such excuses will fail to serve you well during a crisis. There is no better substitute for having a high quality IFAK during an emergency requiring immediate and effective treatment especially if advanced medical help is not coming. Ultimately you have to decide what components to put in your kit and must accept the consequences if you choose not to have a comprehensive IFAK or if you choose not to carry a kit at all. When an emergency happens you are either prepared or you are not as there is very little middle ground. If someone is rapidly bleeding to death you must take immediate action to save their life.

IFAK Components

As previously stated there are many commercially available IFAK's. Some are small and compact but lack necessary items such as a quality tourniquet, an occlusive dressing, or hemostatic agent. A comprehensive kit is larger and more expensive but will effectively treat major traumatic injuries from a gunshot wound or a severe cut from an edged weapon. At a minimum an IFAK must be able to effectively and quickly address severe hemorrhage to an extremity which is the leading causes of death. Below I will list items that I believe are important components that should be considered for your IFAK. Do your own research and obtain items that fit your needs and your level of training.

> *Any IFAK that you consider will be a compromise between carryability and effectiveness of the components. The key is to be able to balance the size of your IFAK with effective and efficient medical components based on your training.*

Following are components that I believe should be an integral part of an IFAK:

Tourniquet

> *It is possible to bleed to death from an injury to a major artery such as the femoral artery in 3-5 minutes. This means that you must aggressively and effectively stop severe arterial hemorrhaging in a timely manner.*

A high quality tourniquet is essential. I recommend the following tourniquets:

1. Combat Application Tourniquet (C-A-T)

2. SOF Tactical Tourniquet (SOFTT)

3. SWAT-T [Back-up tourniquet]

Recommended Tourniquet: Combat Application Tourniquet (C-A-T). The C-A-T is a one-handed windlass tourniquet that can completely occlude arterial blood flow in both an upper or lower extremity.

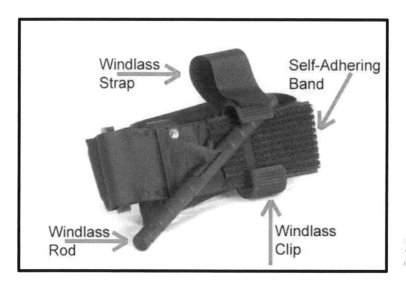

Windlass Strap

Self-Adhering Band

Windlass Rod

Windlass Clip

Tourniquets are used to control <u>severe</u> external hemorrhage from an extremity due to a traumatic injury such as a gunshot wound, knife wound, explosive device, or amputation. Major bleeding occurs when an artery is cut or damaged which can result in death within 3-5 minutes. Your ability to stop major arterial bleeding is critical even when working in an urban environment and emergency services are available and capable of providing aid in a relatively short period of time. Assuming that paramedics are able to treat you within 5-6 minutes still means that you may have lost a substantial amount of blood leaving you in critical condition. The average adult contains approximately 5 liters of blood so it is important to keep every precious drop of blood in your body. An arterial bleed is evidenced by bright red blood that spurts out while a venous bleed is dark in color and flows out but does not spurt. Arteries carry oxygenated blood throughout the body while veins carry deoxygenated blood back to the lungs to pick up oxygen. The major artery in the arm is the brachial artery and the major artery in the leg is the femoral artery.

Bleeding Control

- The leading cause of Death on the battlefield is uncontrolled extremity bleeding.

- In most situations a pressure dressing is adequate to control bleeding—but in "Care Under Fire" you don't have the luxury of time.

  - *Care Under Fire means there is still an active threat*

  - *Think "Active Shooter"*

- In care under fire, a Tourniquet can be applied quickly, and once you have time to properly evaluate the wound, a pressure dressing may replace the tourniquet.

There was a time when utilization of a tourniquet was the last possible option which was highly discouraged and the belief was that the limb would be lost although a life would be saved. Much research has been done which clearly indicates that this is not the case and that tourniquets can be used in a safe manner over a prolonged period of time (6+ hours) without limb damage. There is a well-documented case of tourniquet application that was applied for 16 continuous hours without loss of the limb. According to a study on tourniquet use on combat casualties it states:

"Of tourniquets evaluated in this work, the CAT is the best prehospital tourniquet...[ix]**"**

Another study on the same incident states:

"Tourniquet use for 1 to 3 hours during surgical procedures is commonplace and carries a very low risk of complications. However, it is generally thought that skeletal muscle cannot tolerate ischemia for more than 6 hours without complete loss of viability. It is therefore notable that in the present case, limb salvage was successful after more than 16 hours of tourniquet-induced ischemia.[x]*"*

According to Dr. Lance Stuke[xi] he states the following:

- *"Prehospital tourniquets are indicated if direct pressure or a pressure dressing fails to control hemorrhage.*

- *The tourniquet should be placed prior to extrication and prior to transport. There is a clear survival advantage if placement is done prior to the onset of shock.*

- *There are few, if any, significant complications attributed to tourniquet use. It is a safe procedure, should be performed by all EMS personnel, and saves lives."*

The above information regarding tourniquets should provide you confidence in using them when indicated. The risk of complications is obviously outweighed by the benefits. Early tourniquet use to control severe hemorrhage before shock sets in is clearly advantageous to saving the patient.

Remember that in a Care Under Fire situation you will only address severe extremity bleeding and that tourniquet application is your first choice of control for such life-threatening bleeding. Do not attempt direct pressure, pressure dressing, or any other type of hemorrhage control. Go directly to a tourniquet to control life-threatening bleeding. **Survival rates are improved when tourniquets are applied before the patient goes into shock.** This is an extremely important aspect as once the patient goes into shock their prognosis for a favorable outcome diminishes. According to Walters, Ph.D.[xii]:

"If a soldier is wounded under fire, a tourniquet should be used for any severely bleeding extremity wound. While under fire, the use of direct pressure, pressure dressings, pressure points and elevation may place the casualty and medic at additional risk of injury."

The same article states:

"Regardless of the conditions under which a tourniquet is applied, the most effective method of limb salvage is the early, successful conversion of a tourniquet to a less damaging means of hemorrhage control."

The same applies to civilians when help is delayed and you are in the worst case scenario. You do not need to be on the battlefield to benefit from appropriate use of a tourniquet to save a life. It is important to reiterate that tourniquets should **not** be used for wounds with minor bleeding. Non-life-threatening bleeding should be ignored until the Tactical Field Care phase.

Tourniquets are to be applied approximately 2-3 inches above the wound and never placed directly on the wound. Tourniquets should not be placed directly over the knee or elbow. The tourniquet can be placed over clothing if necessary but it is best if clothing is removed. Do not place a tourniquet over a cargo pocket that contains bulky items. Once applied the distal pulse should be check to verify that the tourniquet is tight enough. If you still can feel a pulse then tighten the tourniquet more. A second tourniquet can be applied directly above the first tourniquet to control bleeding.

Common mistakes with tourniquet application include:

- Failure to apply a tourniquet when it is needed

- Waiting too long to apply the tourniquet and the individual goes into shock

- Failure to tighten it enough to eliminate the distal pulse

- Utilizing a tourniquet for minimal bleeding that does not require a tourniquet

- Applying the tourniquet too high on the limb

- Removing the tourniquet prematurely (generally you will have a medical professional remove the tourniquet at a medical facility)

When utilizing a tourniquet pain and discomfort is to be expected. It is important to understand that pain and discomfort does not indicate that the tourniquet was incorrectly applied and it does not mean that it should be removed. Utilization of a tourniquet is necessary to save a life. It is critical that all severe bleeding be stopped.

Tourniquet

- Attach notation to patient alerting other providers that a tourniquet has been applied.

Write the time the tourniquet was applied.

Too many times I hear people say they will improvise a tourniquet from a shirt, belt or other items.

My question to them is:

Do you really want to improvise such an item under the worst possible conditions when someone's life is on the line?

It is ridiculous to resort to improvising a tourniquet when so many quality ones are commercially available. There is no reason to make a bad situation more stressful when you can just buy a quality tourniquet. You should still know how to improvise a tourniquet but doing so should be your last resort. According to an article in Military Medicine, *"Improvised tourniquet effectiveness was less than that of well-designed tourniquets but was better than not using a tourniquet at all.*[xiii]*"*

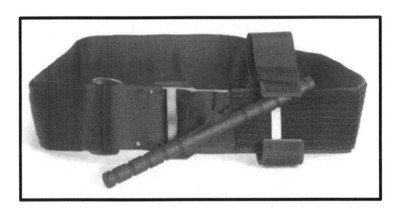

Why the Combat Application Tourniquet?

Based upon research from the United States Army Institute of
Surgical Research Battlefield Tourniquet Recommendations –
Issued July 28, 2004:

*"The Combat Application Tourniquet (C-A-T) was
effective 100% of the time in quickly and effectively
occluding arterial blood flow in both the upper and lower
extremities in all trials...Pain scores (pinching and
circumferential) were dramatically lower with the C-A-T
than any other strap-style device evaluated."*

Performance Steps when using a C-A-T:

1. Remove the C-A-T from the carrying pouch.

2. Slide the extremity through the loop of the Self-Adhering Band or wrap Self-Adhering Band around the extremity and reattach to friction adapter buckle.

3. Position the C-A-T above the wound; leave at least 2 inches of uninjured skin between the C-A-T and the wound.

4. Secure the C-A-T

   - Pull the free running end of the Self-Adhering Band tight and securely fasten it back on itself (if applying to an arm wound). Do not adhere the band past the Windlass Clip.

- If applying to a leg wound, the Self-Adhering Band must be routed through both sides of the friction adapter buckle and fastened back on itself. This will prevent it from loosening when twisting the Windlass Clip.

5. Twist the Windlass Rod until the bleeding stops. When the tactical situation permits insure the distal pulse is no longer palpable.

6. Lock the rod in place with the Windlass Clip.

   NOTE: For added security (and always before moving the casualty), secure the Windlass Rod with the Windlass Strap. For smaller extremities, continue to wind the Self-Adhering Band across the Windlass Clip and secure it under the Windlass Strap.

7. Grasp the Windlass Strap, pull it tight and adhere it to the Velcro on the Windlass Clip.

8. Release and remove the tourniquet. [Training environment]

9. Note that on a real casualty, the date and time the C-A-T was applied would be recorded when tactically feasible.

10. Note that a wound to a real casualty would be dressed, and the casualty would be transported to definitive treatment as dictated by the situation.

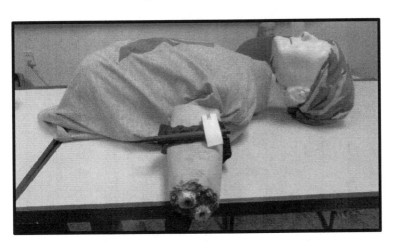

As a back up to the Combat Application Tourniquet I also recommend carrying a SWAT-T[xiv] which is an inexpensive and multipurpose tourniquet that is pretty effective. SWAT stands for **S**tretch, **W**rap **A**nd **T**uck. While it is a tourniquet is will also function as a:

- Pressure dressing for non-arterial bleeds.

- Elastic wrap for sprains or strains. It can also be used to hold ice on an injury.

- Splinting to secure limbs to rigid splints.

At first I was very hesitant and doubtful regarding the effectiveness of the SWAT-T Tourniquet. After attending training with an emergency room physician who demonstrated the use and effectiveness of this tourniquet I was impressed with this product. This is a versatile and effective tourniquet to stop a severe arterial bleed. I will state that my primary tourniquet remains the Combat Application Tourniquet, C-A-T and the SWAT-T is my backup.

Aspects about the SWAT-T that I like:

- Effective which is my primary requirement as it must stop arterial bleeding

- Very durable and will work well in multiple environments from hot to cold

- Extremely light and compact - there is no reason not to carry this tourniquet

- Multipurpose and Versatile - can be used as a tourniquet, sling, and pressure dressing

- Latex free

- Long expiration date

- This tourniquet can be washed and re-used although I probably would not reuse

- Requires very little training to become proficient in its correct application

- Can be applied very high up on a limb

- Reasonably priced

- Very lightweight

Again, I was very surprised to see just how effective this tourniquet is and how easy it is to apply to both large and thin individuals. It is also very easy to learn how to properly apply the SWAT-T. The bottom line is that this tourniquet does work and is effective. If you are looking for an alternative to a larger and more bulky tourniquet then the SWAT-T is a great option. It does not take up much room and will easily fit in a back pocket, shirt pocket, and BDU pocket.

Hemostatic Agent

Hemostatic agents are used on bleeding that is not amenable to tourniquet application. This simply means that a tourniquet cannot be applied based on the location (head, neck, torso, and groin) or type of the injury. There are many different types and brands of hemostatic agents currently available. New and more effective agents are currently being researched.

I recommend the following hemostatic agent:

1. QuikClot Combat Gauze

According to the QuikClot website[xv]:

"After extensive testing by the United States Army Institute for Surgical Research (USAISR) and the Naval Medical Research Center (NMRC), the Committee on Tactical Combat Casualty Care (CoTCCC) chose QuikClot Combat Gauze® as the hemostatic dressing of choice on the battlefield for compressible hemorrhage not amenable to tourniquet use or as an adjunct to tourniquet removal if evacuation time is anticipated to be longer than 2 hours[xvi]. Since its adoption by the US military, more than 5 million units of QuikClot Combat Gauze® have been shipped, and no product-related adverse reactions have been reported."

Again, I hear a lot of people complain about hemostatic agents because they tend to be an expensive component and they have an expiration date. Your patient may also have an expiration date if you cannot stop the bleeding. A quality kit costs more for a reason. When my life or the life of a loved one is on the line I am willing to pay a little more to make sure that we have the best chance for survival. Spending $30-$50 on a quality hemostatic agent is much less expensive than losing a loved one who bleeds to death because I didn't want to spend the money.

Many hemostatic agents will last for three years before they expire. If you use it one time it will be worth its weight in gold. If you never have to use it that is even better. I would rather have this product and not need it than need it and not have it!

Proper Use of Combat Gauze

Step 1: Expose wound & identify bleeding

- Open clothing around the wound.

- If possible, remove excess pooled blood from the wound while preserving any clots already formed in the wound.

- Locate the source of the most active bleeding.

Step 2: Pack wound completely

- Pack it tightly into wound and directly onto the source of bleeding.

- More than one gauze may be required to stem blood flow.

- Combat Gauze may be re-packed or adjusted in the wound to ensure proper placement.

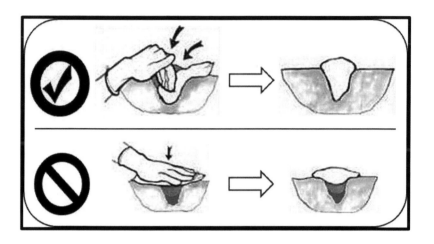

Step 3: Apply direct pressure

- Quickly apply pressure until bleeding stops.

- Hold continuous pressure for 3 minutes.

- Reassess to ensure bleeding is controlled.

- Combat Gauze may be repacked or a second gauze used if initial application fails to provide hemostasis.

Step 4: Bandage over Combat Gauze

- Leave Combat Gauze in place.

- Wrap to effectively secure the dressing in the wound.

Performance Steps:

1. Expose the injury by opening or cutting away the patient's clothing.

2. If possible, remove excess blood from the wound while preserving any clots that may have formed.

3. Locate the source of the most active bleeding.

4. Remove the hemostatic dressing from its sterile package and pack it tightly into the wound directly over the site of the most active bleeding.

5. More than one dressing may be required to control the hemorrhage.

6. Apply direct pressure quickly with enough force to stop the bleeding.

7. **Hold direct pressure for a minimum of 3 minutes.**

8. Reassess for bleeding control.

9. More dressing may be packed into the wound as necessary to stop any continued bleeding.

10. Leave the dressing in place.

11. Secure the hemostatic dressing in place with a pressure dressing.

Another hemostatic agent that is gaining popularity is HemCon ChitoGauze® PRO which also has antibacterial properties to provide effective against a wide range of microorganisms including MRSA, VRE, and Acinetobacter Baumannii.

According to the HemCon website[xvii]:

"What is the ChitoGauze PRO/GuardaCare PRO composition?

The HemCon dressing is composed of a polyester/rayon blend non-woven medical gauze that is coated with chitosan. Chitosan is a naturally occurring, biocompatible polysaccharide derived from shrimp shells. The shrimp shells are processed and chemically treated. Once the gauze is coated with chitosan and packaged to final configuration, they are sterilized. Our chitosan is derived from Pandalus borealis (also called Pandalus eous), the species of shrimp found in cold parts of the North Atlantic Ocean.

Is there a problem using this product on people with shrimp or shellfish allergies?

There have been no known allergic reactions / anaphylaxis as a result of using the HemCon ChitoGauze PRO since distribution began in 2003 and there have been no adverse effects reported in over one million bandages shipped.

To further support the assertion that shrimp allergic individuals are not put at increased risk when using this product, HemCon conducted a clinical study among presumed shrimp-allergic subjects to determine if chitosan can induce immediate wheal reactions indicative of this allergy. A total of 51 subjects were enrolled as subjects known or suspected to be allergic to shrimp were tested. The study concluded that shrimp allergic individuals are not put at increased risk when using this product."

Hemostatic Agent

Recommended Hemostatic Agent is the QuikClot Combat Gauze. This product does not produce heat as some of the older hemostatic agents. QuikClot Combat Gauze is highly effective in stopping bleeding, is safe, has no known contraindications, and has a three year self-life. This product is simple and easy to use with the added benefit that the product instructions are written directly on the package. When using a hemostatic agent such as QuikClot Combat Gauze it is critical to apply direct pressure for a minimum of three minutes.

Pressure Dressing

Pressure dressings must have the ability to actually exert pressure on the wound to assist with stopping the bleeding. They can also function as an improvised tourniquet, wrap, or sling to immobilize an appendage.

I recommend the following pressure dressings:

1. Emergency Trauma Dressing, 4 or 6 inch by North American Rescue

2. Israeli Bandage (Israeli Battle Dressing), 4 or 6 inch

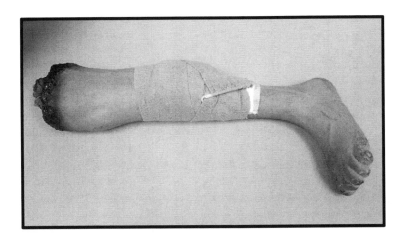

Pressure dressings are another item that people try to skimp on. They are under the false belief that a tampon will do the trick and replace the need for a pressure dressing and/or a hemostatic agent. No, tampons will NOT work with a severe arterial bleed and they are not a substitute for a pressure dressing or a hemostatic agent. Tampons are designed to soak up blood not control bleeding. Pressure dressings are not an expensive item so spend the money and get a few to have in your kit.

Pressure Dressing

Recommended Pressure Dressings are the Emergency Trauma Dressing (ETD), 4 or 6 inch by North American Rescue and the Israeli Bandage. These are sterile dressings used for applying direct pressure. The North American Rescue website has a video of proper use of this pressure dressing which is viewable at: http://www.narescue.com/

Regarding the Israeli Bandage the Israeli First Aid website states[xviii]:

Ease of Operation

The Emergency Bandage has efficient blood staunching capability and offers ease of operation:

1. *The sterile, non-adherent pad is placed on the wound.*

2. *The application of immediate direct pressure to the wound site is achieved by*

wrapping the elasticized woven leader over the topside of the bandage pad where the specially designed pressure bar is situated. The pressure bar is designed to readily accept and hold the wrapping leader.

3. *After engagement of the pressure bar, wrapping the leader in any direction around the limb or body part and onto the pressure bar forces the pressure bar down onto the pad creating the direct pressure needed to bring about homeostasis.*

4. *In addition to its primary function, the pressure bar also facilitates bandaging. The elastic bandage uses the rigid shape of the pressure bar to change direction while bandaging, thus affording the caregiver more options for effective dressing of the wound.*

5. *Subsequent wrappings of the leader secures and maintains the pad in place over the wound, and by covering all the edges of the pad acts as a sterile secondary dressing. The bandage leader is woven to remain at its full width and will not bunch up or twist itself into a rope.*

6. *The closure system of the bandage is*

multi-functional yet simple, quick, and familiar. Situated at the end of the leader is a closure bar (dowel with hooking clips) at each end to secure the wrapping leader the same way that a pen is secured in a shirt pocket. The closure bar holds the bandage securely in place over the wound site.

7. *If additional pressure is required the closure bar is easily removed from its first closure position and inserted between previous layers of the leader directly above the protruding pressure bar and rotated. This rotation of the closure bar acts to further press down the pressure bar onto the wound to exert blood-staunching pressure. The closure bar is used as before to secure the dressing.*

Evisceration

An abdominal evisceration is a serious injury where part of the intestines or other internal organ is protruding outside of the abdominal cavity through an open wound. In such cases you do **NOT** want to attempt to put the organs or tissue back into the abdominal cavity.

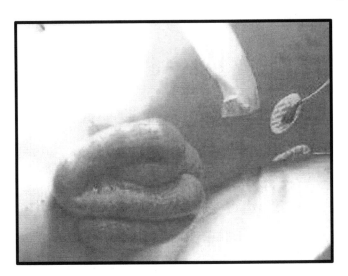

The focus should be on protecting the intestine or other organs from further damage. It is also important that the contents are covered with a sterile dressing that is moistened, preferable with sterile saline, to protect the organs from drying which will result in cell death. The dressing may need to be remoistened periodically. There is no need to exert pressure on the dressing. There are companies that specifically make abdominal dressings which work well for eviscerations.

Things to keep in mind when treating an abdominal evisceration:

- If necessary, carefully scoop up the eviscerated organ using a saturated saline dressing and do not directly handle the eviscerated parts with hands or unsterile objects due to an increased risk of infection.

- Do not attempt to replace eviscerated organs into the abdominal cavity. Instead, cover them with a saturated sterile dressing or an air tight non-adhering dressing to prevent the intestines from drying.

- Do not use tap water to saturate dressings. Use only normal saline for dressings. Water is a hypotonic solution and water diffuses into the cells and when the cell volume exceeds the cell capacity it will burst.

- Keep eviscerated organs saturated and warm since organ dehydration and heat loss occurs rapidly with an open abdominal cavity. Place towels or occlusive dressings over the dressings already applied.

- Re-saturate dressings as needed to prevent dressings from becoming dry and adhering to abdominal organs/tissue resulting in additional cellular destruction and necrosis (tissue death.)

- Unless contraindicated bend the patients knees to decreases tension on abdominal muscles. Use a pillow under the patient's knees to keep them flexed and to provide comfort for the patient.

- Occlusive dressings consist of plastic wrap or sheeting or additional dry dressings over the saturated dressing. Do not use aluminum foil, this may cause cuts or further damage of the eviscerated organ.

- Secure dressings by taping around all sides or tying cravats above and below the position of the exposed eviscerated organ.

Because this is such a serious injury the patient will oftentimes be very panicked and frightened. It is important to provide support in an attempt to keep the patient as calm as possible. The only solution to an evisceration is surgery. It's vital to organ survival that organs remain covered and moist until the patient obtains surgical care.

Chest Seal

Rapid treatment of an open pneumothorax (sucking chest wound) consists of forming a seal over the wound which will help the patient breathe easier. A patient with an open pneumothorax will generally exhibit obvious respiratory distress, will be anxious and have a rapid heart rate. It is important to check for both an entrance and an exit wound. The initial treatment for an open pneumothorax involves sealing the defect in the chest wall.

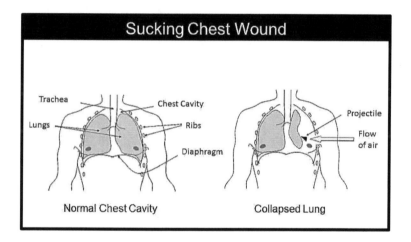

Signs and Symptoms of an Open Chest Wound include:

- Obvious penetration of the chest cavity
- Shortness of breath
- Difficulty breathing

- Sucking sound coming from the chest wound
- Frothy blood from the chest wound
- Pain in the chest or shoulder area which increases with breathing
- Chest not rising normally when the patient inhales
- Rapid and weak heartbeat
- Cyanotic (blueish) tint to lips, inside of mouth and nailbeds.

I recommend the following chest seals:

1. Hyfin Vent Chest Seal

2. Asherman Chest Seal

3. Bolin Chest Seal

According to research published in the Journal of Special Operations Medicine[xix]:

> *"All open and/or sucking chest wounds should be treated by immediately applying a vented chest seal to cover the defect. If a vented chest seal is not available, use a non-vented chest*

seal. Monitor the casualty for the potential development of a subsequent tension pneumothorax. If the casualty develops increasing hypoxia, respiratory distress, or hypotension and a tension pneumothorax is suspected, treat by burping or removing the dressing or by needle decompression."

In a situation where you do not have a commercially available chest seal it is possible to improvise one in the field. Clean the chest area as best you can of all blood or fluids. Then tape a piece of aluminum foil or plastic wrap to the chest wall on three sides. This will create a flutter valve effect which allows air to escape from the pleural space but not enter into it. If you have petroleum impregnated gauze this will also work. If the patient has increased difficulty in breathing, shortness of breath, or is cyanotic you should then lift the seal (if it does not have a vent) to let the air escape with complete expiration, and then reseal the wound. Again, I stress that it is always better to have commercially available medical equipment when possible.

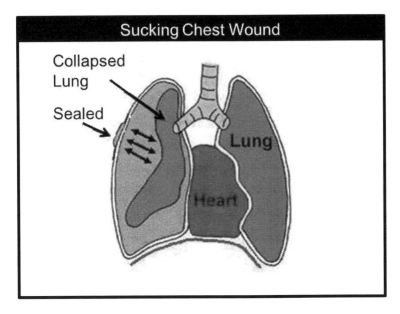

Remember that a tension pneumothorax may develop which is a life-threatening condition. Patients who have tension pneumothorax will usually present with difficulty breathing and chest pain. As the tension progresses so does difficulty in breathing. If this process continues the patient may turn cyanotic and may stop breathing. So much pressure may be placed on the heart that it is no longer able to pump and the patient expires. The classic signs of a tension pneumothorax are deviation of the trachea away from the side with the tension, a hyper-expanded chest, an increased percussion note and a hyper-expanded chest that moves little with respiration.[xx]

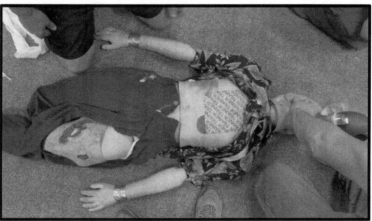

Chest Seal

Recommended is the Hyfin Chest Vent Seal. This seal is a 6"x6" occlusive dressing used for the treatment of penetrating injuries to the chest. The North American Rescue states the following[xxi]:

"The new HyFin Vent Chest Seal from North American Rescue sets the standard for the treatment of penetrating injuries to the chest. The new HyFin Vent Chest Seal design provides 3-vented channels that prevent airflow into the chest cavity during inspiration while allowing air to escape through the vent channels during exhalation. The 3-vent channels allow blood to escape and also provide a backup fail-safe system, as even if two of the three channels become obstructed, the vent will remain fully operational.

Advanced adhesive technology provides superior adhesion in the most adverse conditions, including sweaty or hairy casualties. Packaged in a rugged, easy-to-open foil pouch, the perforated packaging allows rescuers to open only one dressing at a time as needed. Each chest seal also includes a gauze pad to wipe the wound surface prior to application. Each HyFin Vent Chest Seal has a large, Red-Tip ™ pull tab for single-step peel-and-apply application and allows for the burping of the wound if necessary. The clear, transparent backing allows for easy placement over the wound area and conformability to the patient's chest.

Meets or exceeds the current EMS Standard of Care and TCCC & TECC Guidelines for treatment of penetrating injuries to the chest, the new HyFin Vent Chest Seal Twin Pack is the superior prehospital chest seal."

Treatment of an open "sucking" chest wound (open pneumothorax) consists of covering the wound during expiration (breathing out) with an occlusive dressing. An occlusive dressing should extend a minimum of two inches past the edge of the wound to provide the best seal possible. There are many commercially available products that have very functional adhesive properties to seal the wound. Following are some of the more popular chest seals on the market: Hyfin, Asherman, Bolin, and Halo. The wound should be sealed on all four sides and the patient should then be placed in a sitting position if there are no other injuries. Application of an occlusive dressing should improve the patients breathing. The patient should then be monitored for the development of a tension pneumothorax which can result in increasingly difficulty breathing. If a tension pneumothorax develops the injured patient will need a needle decompression which needs to be performed by a person with appropriate medical training.

If there is a knife in the chest or other part of the body do not remove it. Leave in in place and attempt to secure it with dressings so that the knife does not move and cause further injury.

The North American Rescue website has a video of proper use of this chest seal which is viewable at: https://www.narescue.com/Video_Downloads.htm

Nasopharyngeal Airway (NPA)

A nasopharyngeal airway is to be used on an unconscious or semi-conscious individual who is unable to maintain an airway. Use of an NPA typically requires formal training and should not be used without such training.

I recommend the following NPA:

Nasopharyngeal Airway (28 Fr.) with Surgilube by Rusch (Note: *There are different size NPA's available and the 28 Fr. is a common size among adults. It should not be used on juveniles.*)

Nasopharyngeal Airway (NPA)

If spontaneous respirations are present without respiratory distress, an adequate airway in the **unconscious** casualty is best maintained with a nasopharyngeal airway (NPA).

After inserting the NPA, place the casualty in the recovery position to maintain the open airway and prevent aspiration of blood, mucous, or vomitus.

Contraindications for using a Nasopharyngeal Airway (NPA)

1. Any evidence of a head injury or roof of mouth fracture; the airway may inadvertently enter the cranial vault with this type fracture

2. Exposed brain matter

3. Cerebrospinal fluid (CSF) draining from nose, mouth, or ears

Nasopharyngeal Airway

- Lubricate
- Insert along floor of nasal cavity
- If resistance is met use back and forth motion
- Do NOT force – Use another nostril
- If patient gags, withdraw slightly

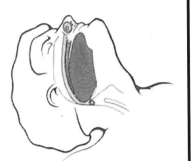

Performance Steps for use of a NPA:

1. Assemble all necessary equipment.

2. Assess the upper airway for visible obstruction.

3. Open the airway with a chin lift/jaw thrust maneuver.

4. Lubricate the Nasopharyngeal Airway with a surgical lubricant.

5. Insert the airway into the nose at a 90 degree angle to the face. Avoid aiming upwards towards the top of the head. Insert all the way to the flange.

6. Use a rotary and/or back-and-forth motion to facilitate insertion.

7. If unable to insert on one side of the nasal passage, take it out and try the other side.

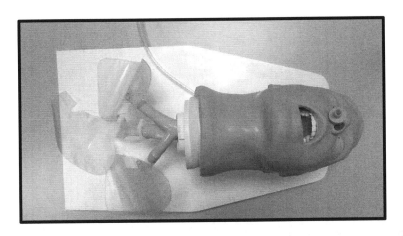

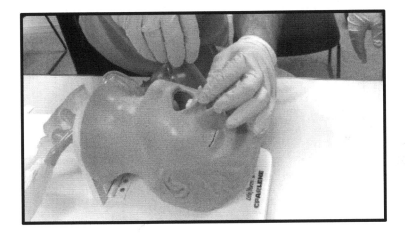

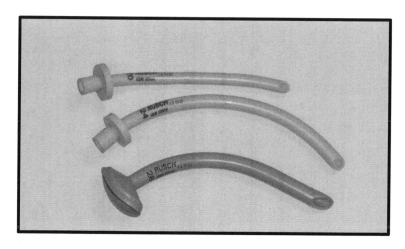

Nasopharyngeal Airway (NPA)

    While insertion of a Nasopharyngeal Airway is not a difficult skill it is also best that you receive professional hands on training in its application. It is also important to know that there are some contraindications for using a NPA which will be covered in training.

Gloves

Gloves are essential to provide protection from bloodborne pathogens such as hepatitis, HIV/AIDS, and others. Always wear gloves when working around all body fluids and keep in mind that there are other body fluids besides blood which can contain pathogens. Assume all blood, body fluids and tissues are potentially infectious and take appropriate measures to safely handle these body substances which is known as Universal Precautions. Such body fluids can be: Peritoneal fluid, cerebrospinal fluid, synovial fluid, pleural fluid, pericardial fluid, vomit/feces, saliva, amniotic fluid, vaginal secretions and semen. If you do not know what it is then consider it as other potentially infectious material and take appropriate precautions. There is no reason for you to become infected with a potentially life-threatening disease when providing care for others.

I recommend the following personal protective gloves:

Black Talon Nitrile Gloves

I like the Black Talon Nitrile Gloves because they fit well, are durable, and still allow for tactile sensation. Regardless of which types of gloves that you use never expose them to heat for an extended period of time or the gloves will be more likely to tear. Always carry more than one pair of gloves should a glove rip or you need to treat multiple victims. Replace gloves that are stored in your kit on an annual basis.

Shock

When treating a patient always be on the lookout for shock which can rapidly deteriorate the patient's condition leading to death. The definition of shock can be a very complicated topic as it is very encompassing. To keep things very basic shock will be defined as a *lack of tissue perfusion to support life*. Essentially the cells are not getting enough oxygen to survive which eventually leads to systemic failure of the organs to include the brain and heart.

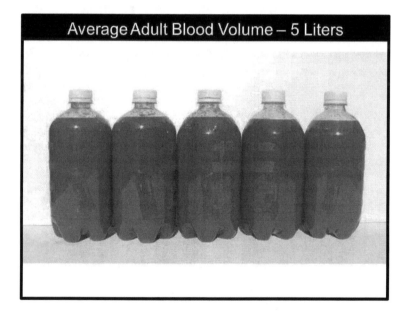
Average Adult Blood Volume – 5 Liters

The average blood volume of an adult is 5-6 liters. A loss of 25%-40% of the person's total blood volume will create a life-threatening condition. Keep in mind that internal bleeding generally needs to be fixed by a surgeon in an operating room and there is not much you can do in the field to address such bleeding.

Signs and Symptoms of Shock

- Altered mental status
- Pale, cool, clammy skin
- Nausea and vomiting
- Vital sign changes
- Restlessness, anxiety
- Extreme thirst
- Rapid, weak pulse
- Rapid, shallow respirations
- Decreased blood pressure (late sign)

Management of shock, especially due to traumatic injury, is difficult without advanced medical care and proper medical supplies. The best you can do to treat shock is:

- Insure there is an adequate airway
- Control external bleeding
- Maintain body heat

- Transport the patient to an appropriate medical facility as soon as possible

When Help is Delayed

In a *"worst case scenario"* help may be delayed for hours, days, or indefinitely. When help is going to be significantly delayed the chances of a positive outcome decrease meaning that you may lose the patient or the patient may end up with a life-long disability due to the injury. You may end up going from a care giver to a more supportive role especially if there is nothing that you can do medically for the patient. In this difficult situation do your best to provide comfort to the person who is going to die. It may not seem like you are doing enough but it is a kind gesture that does matter and it has meaning. Potentially you can reassure the patient's family members that you did everything possible and that their loved one did not die alone.

Following are some factors to keep in mind anytime that help is delayed for an unknown period of time.

Bleeding

Arterial bleeding is always a life threatening situation as a person can die within minutes as a result of their injury. But, when help is delayed even venous bleeding can be problematic due to the cumulative effect of blood loss. In such situations it is critical to stop all bleeding. Direct pressure applied for 10-15 minutes on the bleeding site and then application of a pressure dressing tends to be effective. Every drop of blood is precious and functions better inside your body than outside your body.

> **Bottom line:** ***Stop all bleeding when help is delayed.***

Infection Prevention

Wounds that are contaminated by dirt, debris, and other items are often cleaned in the emergency department with high pressure irrigation. You are not going to have the ability to provide this level of wound cleaning. Infections can occur quickly becoming a serious condition when help is delayed. Anytime that help is going to be delayed the wound should be cleaned. This can be accomplished by irrigating the wound to remove bacteria. Using water that is clean enough to drink will work in this situation. If you use water from a stream or melted snow it is best to treat the water first using whatever method you use to make water drinkable. When possible, it is best to irrigate the wound with some pressure from a bulb syringe or better yet a 35 ml syringe with an 18 gauge needle. The goal is to squirt the water throughout the wound using the pressure to clean it. Remember, that this may cause blood to get on you so it is important to use protective measures such as gloves and googles. You may need to use a gauze pad to clean out the wound which may be painful. Once the wound is irrigated you want to dress and bandage the wound. It is good practice to change the dressing daily. Remember, it is about doing the best you can with what you have in your medical kit.

It is also recommended that you talk with your primary care physician about having a supply on hand of antibiotics for such a situation. Your physician will let you know which antibiotic is the best for you based on your medical history.

Cardiopulmonary Resuscitation

If a patient receives a traumatic injury and has no pulse or respirations and help is going to be delayed then CPR is not indicated. It is a hard reality that the patient is not going to survive regardless of what actions you initiate. This is especially difficult if the patient is a loved one. Traumatic cardiac arrest has a poor prognosis even under the best medical conditions. When help is delayed there really is no chance of saving the individual. In such a situation you may need to be strong for other family members. This does not mean that you will not grieve for your loss you will just put that grief on hold until you and your group are safe and out of immediate danger.

Coping with Loss

People die. Loved ones die. Children die. Friends die. Death is inevitable for all of us. Death does not discriminate and all of us will eventually face the same fate. Under the best circumstances death can dramatically tax our coping mechanisms. When death comes from trauma and/or violence it can be even more challenging. When you are the person attempting to treat an individual or individuals who have suffered a severe traumatic injury there is always the possibility that the person is going to die. This is an inescapable reality.

Years ago I was an Emergency Medical Technician (EMT) and I have seen my share of death. It did not take me long to come to the stark realization that people will die despite my best efforts. I have seen patients die in trauma bays in top rated Level 1 trauma hospitals with the best medical care available. Seeing death up close and personal made me realize that people can and will die no matter what level of care they receive. This does not mean that I would not provide the best care possible it just means that despite the best care some people cannot be saved. For me it came to a point where I had to accept this reality. It also helped me to cope with patients that did not survive. I knew I did everything possible and this was beneficial for my psychological health as I did not take their death personally. You may find yourself in a situation where you do everything you can to help a person and they still do not survive. If this occurs it is important to know that you did everything possible with the level of training, skills, and equipment that you had with you. Never place unrealistic expectations on yourself and believe that you can save everyone. This is setting yourself up for failure and even the best trauma surgeon loses patients. What can make this situation exponentially more difficult is the person you lose may be a family member such as a spouse or child. There is no easy way around the grief that you will encounter. My best recommendation is to seek appropriate psychological help from a mental health professional. Grief counseling is very effective and can help you resolve any difficulties that you may end up facing. This is not to say that your road to healing will be easy but it will be worth it. It is also important to surround yourself with a support network.

Summary

When referring to IFAK components keep in mind that the above list is subject to change based on new products that are developed or current products that are improved. It is important to conduct some research to find which components will suit your needs best, receive training from a qualified source, train with your IFAK so that you are familiar with each item that you carry and keep current on new advancements and products. You can also purchase a pre-made commercially available IFAK and modify it to your needs. It is extremely important to keep current with your medical skills.

Summary

Training for the worst case scenario is a must. Individuals need the knowledge, skills, and abilities to know what type of care to provide in a crisis. This will give you an increased chance of saving lives especially when time is of the essence. Having medical skills will also boost your confidence that you have the training to take care of yourself and loved ones in an emergency. A severe hemorrhage can lead to death within a matter of minutes. Your ability to provide self-care and care for others may be what keeps you alive until a higher level of medical care can assist. Attend training that goes into more depth than basic first aid and CPR. Basic first aid training is really training geared toward the best case scenario while care under fire training is the training for the worst case scenario. You must not only have the skills to treat severe bleeding and chest wounds but you must also carry a quality Individual First Aid Kit (IFAK) on your person. It is possible to spend a lot of money on a quality IFAK but it is impossible to put a price on the life that you may safe. This is especially true if the person you save is a family member, loved one or friend.

Considering that trauma is the #1 cause of death for Americans between 1 and 44 years old it makes good sense to have some knowledge in dealing with such injuries. Being confident in your abilities will provide you with peace of mind because you know that you possess lifesaving skills.

Basic skills that you must obtain and perfect include:

- Patient Assessment

- Personal Protective Equipment

- Tourniquet Application

- Hemostatic Agent

- Chest Seal Application

- Nasopharyngeal Airway Insertion

- Pressure Dressing

- Signs and symptoms of shock

Having knowledge of these skills and how to properly use them will provide you with a significant amount of abilities to treat the wounded in a crises or emergency situation. Life is full of unknowns which is evident by the numerous terrorist attacks that occur on a regular basis throughout the world. Even if you think terrorism is a low probably for you the truth is the simple act of getting in a vehicle is a real potential source of traumatic injury. This is why it is important to take preventive measure when engaging in certain activities. In a vehicle wear your seatbelt properly and focus on driving. Too many drivers are distracted by cell phones which leads to many accidents. Never text and operate a motor vehicle. If you ride a motorcycle wear a helmet and protective clothing. Don't drink and drive or use certain prescription medications and drive. Many individuals are under the false belief that they can take prescription medications and drive. Many states have laws against driving under the influence of prescription medications such as narcotics, muscle relaxers, anti-anxiety medication and others. Even when you take your prescription medication as prescribed by your doctor you can still get arrested for impaired driving.

Reading Trauma Care for the Worst Case Scenario, 2nd Edition is not and never will be a substitute for receiving hands on training. In order to keep skills relevant you must practice and keep up to date. You cannot do that from a book. This book is a resource that must be used in conjunction with training and practice. It is my hope that you never have to use any of the skills presented in this book.

Practical Exercises

Following are a list of practical exercises to expose you to some of the concepts in this book. Each scenario can be modified in any way that meets your needs. The exercises are relatively basic and not every possible function is covered.

These exercises should be performed under proper medical and tactical guidance. I cannot stress enough the importance of receiving proper medical training on first aid, CPR, CCR, AED, and use of a tourniquet, nasopharyngeal airway, chest seal, hemostatic agents and pressure dressing.

Never perform medical care that is above your level of training as you are placing the patient in danger and can potentially be held liable for your actions.

Remember the mantra: **Do no harm.**

Trauma Care for the Worst Case Scenario, 2nd Edition

Good Samaritan Laws

Protect people against claims of negligence when they give emergency care in good faith without accepting anything in return. Good Samaritan laws usually protect citizens who act the same way that a "*reasonable and prudent person*" would if that person were in the same situation.

For example, a reasonable and prudent person would:

- Move a person only if the person's life were in danger
- Ask a conscious person for permission, also called consent, before giving care
- Check the person for life-threatening conditions before giving further care
- Call 9-1-1 or the local emergency number
- Continue to give care until more highly trained personnel take over

American Red Cross

126

Practical Exercise 1: Evaluation Sheet

Scenario:

> In this scenario you and your wife are walking down a busy city street in a major metropolitan city.
>
> As you are walking a young thug comes behind your wife and attempts to steal her purse by using a knife to cut the strap. Instead of cutting the strap he slashes your wife in her right bicep and it is now spurting bright red blood.
>
> The offender runs away and is quickly out of sight and no longer a threat to your safety.
>
> What action do you take?

Available Gear:

> Tourniquet, pressure dressing, hemostatic agent, nasopharyngeal airway, chest seal, nitrile gloves, and cell phone

Performance Activities:

- Directs someone to immediately call 9-1-1?
- Performs an accurate patient assessment?
- Does not cause further injury to the patient?
- Rapidly identifies a brachial artery

hemorrhage and utilizes a tourniquet?

- Correctly applied tourniquet?
- Tourniquet properly placed above wound?
- Tourniquet applied until bleeding controlled?
- Application time for applying tourniquet:

_____

Practical Exercise 2: Evaluation Sheet

<u>Scenario:</u>

In this scenario you and your family are driving down a remote freeway which is a minimum of 45 minutes from the nearest town.

You are driving at 70 miles per hour when a blowout occurs to your front tire causing your vehicle to violently swerve multiple times. Fortunately, you prevented the car from rolling over. You and your wife are uninjured but your 15 year old son hit is head on the back seat side window causing it to shatter. The result is a severe laceration to the side of his scalp with bright red blood spurting all over the place. He is conscious, alert, and oriented. He does not complain of any other injuries.

What action do you take?

<u>Available Gear:</u>

Tourniquet, pressure dressing, hemostatic agent, nasopharyngeal airway, chest seal, nitrile gloves, and cell phone

Performance Activities:

- Directs someone to immediately call 9-1-1? (If you have cell service)
- Performs an accurate patient assessment?
- Does not cause further injury to the patient?
- Rapidly identifies an arterial hemorrhage and utilizes a hemostatic agent?
- Correctly applied hemostatic agent?
- Held appropriate pressure for three minutes?
- Used a pressure dressing over the wound and applied it correctly?

Practical Exercise 3: Evaluation Sheet

Scenario:

It is Saturday evening and you are home with your family enjoying the weekend. You walk out to the front yard to put a hose away when a bomb explodes. You have been hit in the chest with a piece of sharp shrapnel. You immediately fall to the ground, grasp your chest, and are having difficulty breathing.

Your wife comes out of the house and you inform her you have a chest wound?

What actions should the wife take?

Available Gear:

Tourniquet, pressure dressing, hemostatic agent, nasopharyngeal airway, chest seal, nitrile gloves, and cell phone

Performance Activities:

- Directs someone to immediately call 9-1-1?
- Moves the husband to a safe location inside the house?
- Performs an accurate patient assessment?
- Does not cause further injury to the patient?

- Rapidly identifies an open chest wound and utilizes a chest seal?
- Correctly applies chest seal?
- Positions the father either in a sitting position or on his side with the injured side next to the ground?
- Monitors for development of a tension pneumothorax?
- Treats for shock?

Practical Exercise 4: Evaluation Sheet

<u>Scenario:</u>

You are at the range practicing one shot draws from the 7 yard line. You are performing well and decide to speed up to get faster hits on target. After shooting the target you attempt to holster your weapon and the weapon discharges one .45 caliber round into your thigh which is now spurting bright red blood.

What action do you take? [Note: You attempt to use a hemostatic agent but it is not effective due to improper application...now what?]

<u>Available Gear:</u>

Tourniquet, pressure dressing, hemostatic agent, nasopharyngeal airway, chest seal, nitrile gloves, and cell phone

<u>Performance Activities:</u>

- Direct someone to immediately call 9-1-1? (If you have cell service)
- Performs an accurate self-assessment?
- Rapidly identifies an artery hemorrhage and utilizes a hemostatic agent?
- Correctly applied hemostatic agent?

- Held appropriate pressure for three minutes?
- Used a pressure dressing over the wound and applied it correctly?
- Correctly applied tourniquet?
- Tourniquet properly placed above wound?
- Tourniquet applied until bleeding controlled?
- Application time for applying tourniquet:

  _____

Practical Exercise 5: Evaluation Sheet

<u>Scenario:</u>

You are at work in a typical urban office environment. An individual comes into your office and randomly starts shooting people. You are not injured but you have multiple co-workers who are seriously injured.

The shooter kills himself and is no longer a threat.

What action do you take?

<u>Available Gear:</u>

Tourniquet, pressure dressing, hemostatic agent, nasopharyngeal airway, chest seal, nitrile gloves, and cell phone

<u>Note:</u>

In this scenario you have limited equipment but multiple serious casualties. You are going to need to determine who you will treat realizing that medical professionals will shortly be on the way. You can modify this scenario by changing certain elements to fit your needs or to add to the complexity of the scenario.

Performance Activities:

- Immediately call 9-1-1?
- Performs triage to see who needs treatment the most?
- Performs an accurate patient assessment?
- Performs appropriate care to include:
  - ➤ _____
  - ➤ _____
  - ➤ _____
  - ➤ _____
  - ➤ _____
  - ➤ _____
  - ➤ _____
  - ➤ _____
  - ➤ _____
  - ➤ _____
  - ➤ _____
  - ➤ _____

Practical Exercise 6: Evaluation Sheet

<u>Scenario:</u>

You are primitive camping with your family in a remote location where you do not receive phone service. Your wife is walking to the truck to get something when she trips and falls to the ground. She is knocked out unconscious from the fall.

- She is not bleeding and does not appear to have any facial or head trauma

- Both pupils are equal

- No fluids are coming out of her nose or ears

- She is breathing on her own

- She has a pulse of 76 beats per minute

What action do you take?

<u>Available Gear:</u>

Tourniquet, pressure dressing, hemostatic agent, nasopharyngeal airway, chest seal, nitrile gloves, and cell phone

Performance Activities:

- Performs an accurate patient assessment?
- Monitors respirations and pulse?
- Considers using an NPA?
- Takes action to prevent shock?
- Keeps patient warm?
- Develops a transport plan to a hospital?

Practical Exercise 7: Evaluation Sheet

Scenario:

> You are at a weekend getaway with a group of
> friends. You are located in a cabin in a very
> small town where cell phone service is spotty
> and unreliable. It is just after dinner time and
> everyone is ready to have some homemade
> pie. One of the guys who is going to cut the pie
> slips on some liquid on the ground and falls.
> He impaled himself with the knife which is in
> his abdomen with only the handle showing.
> The person is writhing in pain.
>
> What action do you take?

Available Gear:

> Tourniquet, pressure dressing, hemostatic
> agent, nasopharyngeal airway, chest seal,
> nitrile gloves, and cell phone

Performance Activities:

- Direct someone to immediately call 9-1-1?
  (If you have cell service)
- Performs an accurate patient assessment?
- Does NOT remove the knife?

- Attempts to stabilize the knife in place?
- Attempts to talk to the patient so that he remains calm considering the circumstances?
- Monitors patient for shock?

Practical Exercise 8: Evaluation Sheet

<u>Scenario:</u>

You are driving down the freeway at 65 MPH. A motorcycle passes you on your left side and speeds off. About a ½ mile down the road you see an accident where it appears that the driver of the motorcycle slammed into the back of a 4 door passenger vehicle. No one in the vehicle appears to be injured. The driver of the motorcycle was wearing a helmet and is completely conscious and alert. The only injury that he has is a compound fracture of his right femur in which his thigh bone is sticking out of his leg. He is profusely bleeding bright red blood that is spurting from the wound.

What action do you take?

<u>Available Gear:</u>

Tourniquet, pressure dressing, hemostatic agent, nasopharyngeal airway, chest seal, nitrile gloves, and cell phone

<u>Performance Activities:</u>

- Direct someone to immediately call 9-1-1? (If you have cell service)

- Performs an accurate patient assessment?
- Rapidly identifies an artery hemorrhage and utilizes a hemostatic agent?
- Cuts away clothing?
- Correctly applied hemostatic agent?
- Held appropriate pressure for three minutes?
- Used a pressure dressing over the wound and applied it correctly?
- Correctly applied tourniquet?
- Tourniquet properly placed above wound?
- Tourniquet applied until bleeding controlled?
- Application time for applying tourniquet:

_____

Practical Exercise 9: Evaluation Sheet

<u>Scenario:</u>

You are on a backpacking trip with your best friend in a remote wilderness area where there is no cell phone reception. You both stop to get a drink of water and to take off your backpacks. As your friend is taking off his backpack he loses his balance and falls. As he is falling he hits that back of his head on a rock. He is profusely bleeding from his head.

- He never lost consciousness. He is alert and oriented and states he is fine.

- Both pupils are equal

- No fluids are coming out of his nose or ears

- He is breathing on his own

- He has a pulse of 64 beats per minute

What action do you take?

<u>Available Gear:</u>

Tourniquet, pressure dressing, hemostatic agent, nasopharyngeal airway, chest seal, nitrile gloves, and cell phone

Performance Activities:

- Performs an accurate patient assessment?
- Palpates the head to check for a potential skull fracture?
- Rapidly identifies a hemorrhage and utilizes a pressure dressing? Pressure dressing is not effective.
- Correctly applied hemostatic agent?
- Had patient hold appropriate pressure for three minutes?
- Used a pressure dressing over the wound and applied it correctly?
- Monitors respirations and pulse?
- Takes action to prevent shock?
- Keeps patient warm?
- What is the decision regarding continuing to move to your destination or setting up camp for the night?
- Develops a transport plan to a hospital if necessary?

Other Scenarios to Consider

Scenarios should not be limited to the examples provided. Feel free to come up with your own examples or modify the previous examples to fit your needs. The following scenarios are purposely generic so that you can fill in the blanks of the scenario. You get to determine the facts of the situation so that the scenario can be used anyway that you see fit. Feel free to change the type of injury, location of the injury, severity, your location and whether help is arriving or not. You can modify the scenarios to take them from the best case scenario to the worst case scenario as you increase your skills and confidence. The key is to train for the worst case scenario so that if you ever encounter such a situation you will not be as impacted by the psychological and physiological reactions to stress. Yes, you will still encounter stress but it should not be so bad that it prevents you from providing necessary care.

Potential scenarios:

1. Improvised explosive device such as the Boston Marathon bombing – treat an amputation. (You can treat yourself or another individual)

2. Injury cause from rioting - treat severe bleeding from a head wound caused by

an individual hit in the head with a stone. No loss of consciousness. How would you treat this person?

3. You come upon a suicide attempt where a young male has seriously slashed his left wrist with a knife and he is bleeding profusely. How would you treat this person?

4. You are at the park with your family. Your son is riding his skateboard and falls with causes an open fracture of his upper right arm. He was wearing a helmet and did not lose consciousness. His arm is bleeding profusely. How would you treat your son?

5. You leave your place of employment and find that activists have been protesting all day and it has turned violent. You safely get to your parking garage and see a female lying on the ground in a pool of blood from a head injury. She is breathing but unconscious.

6. You and your family are deep in a national park watching wildlife and enjoying your vacation. You see other people who are attempting to

photograph bears. One of the individuals gets too close to the bear and gets attacked. He suffers from numerous puncture wounds and a severe bite to his left forearm. After the attack the bears leave the area. There is no cell phone service and no one else is around. How would you treat this person?

7. You are on a remote highway when you see a broken down vehicle with the hood up. Outside the vehicle is two teenage girls yelling and screaming for help. Their father attempted to fix a problem with the engine when something went wrong and two fingers were completely amputated. There is no cell service. How would you treat this person?

8. You are at a sporting event when an earthquake occurs causing severe damage and multiple significant injuries. Your spouse is trapped by a large cement post. She has a severe crush injury to her lower right leg. There is almost no bleeding because the post is holding pressure on the wound. You attempt to call emergency services at 9-

1-1 but your cell phone is not working because the telecommunications network was destroyed. Hundreds if not thousands of people need immediate help. You are on your own for an unforeseeable period of time. What do you do?

9. You are at a concert when a fight breaks out. After the fight is over and the confusion settles there is a young male lying on the ground with a knife impaled in his chest. He is alert and conscious but complains of difficulty breathing. What do you do?

10. You and a group of your friends are camping in a remote area. Out of nowhere you heard a gunshot and one of your friends is shot in the chest from a person hiding in the woods. What do you do?

Resources

Following are resources that you can use to increase your knowledge. These resources are not a substitute for hands on training or certification.

1. *Building a Trauma Kit* by Gunner Morgan

2. *Handbook of First Aid and Emergency Care, Revised Edition* by American Medical Association

3. *Prehospital Trauma Life Support* by NAEMT and American College of Surgeons Committee on Trauma

4. *Tactical Medicine Essentials* by American College of Emergency Physicians (ACEP)

5. *68W Advanced Field Craft: Combat Medic Skills* by United States Army

6. *Medicine for the Outdoors: The Essential Guide to Emergency Medical Procedures and First Aid* by Paul S. Auerbach

7. *The Survival Medicine Handbook: A guide for when help is NOT on the way* by Joseph Alton and Amy Alton

8. *The Survival Doctor's Guide to Wounds: What to Do When There Is No Doctor* by James Hubbard

9. To learn more about Tactical Combat Casualty Care visit:

   http://www.naemt.org/education/TCCC/guidelin es_curriculum.aspx

Final Note

If you found ***Trauma Care for the Worst Case Scenario, 2nd Edition*** beneficial please consider writing a positive review on Amazon so that others may benefit from this work.

Other Works by Gunner Morgan:

- **Building a Trauma Kit**
- **"Reality" in Reality Survival Shows**
- **Practical Defense for the Untrained Person**
- **Psychology of Preppers: Mental Health Issues**

References

i http://www.cdc.gov/injury/index.html

ii http://www.nationaltraumainstitute.org/home/trauma_statistics.html

iii http://www.cdc.gov/injury/overview/data.html

iv http://www.cdc.gov/injury/global/index.html

v http://www.naemt.org/education/PHTLS/TraumaFirstResponse.aspx

vi http://medical-dictionary.thefreedictionary.com/Blunt+Injury

vii http://medical-dictionary.thefreedictionary.com/penetrating+wound

viii Bellamy RF. "The Causes of Death in Conventional Land Warfare: Implications for Combat Casualty Care Research." Mil Med 1984

ix Kragh JF. "Practical Use of Emergency Tourniquets to Stop Bleeding in Major Limb Trauma." The Journal of TRAUMA Injury, Infection, and Critical Care, February Supplement 2008

x Kragh JF. "Extended (16-Hour) Tourniquet Application After Combat Wounds: A Case Report and Review of the Current Literature." Orthop Trauma, Volume 21, Number 4, April 2007

xi Stuke, Lance. "Prehospital Tourniquet Use – A Review of the Current Literature." PHTLS

xii Walters, Ph.D., Thomas. "Issues Related to the Use of Tourniquets on the Battlefield." United States Army Institute of Surgical Research, Combat Casualty Care Research Program

xiii Kragh JF. "The Military Emergency Tourniquet Program's Lessons Learned with Devices and Designs." Military Medicine, Vol 176, October 2011
xiv For more information on the SWAT-T visit their webpage at:
http://www.swattourniquet.com/product.html
xv http://www.quikclot.com/Military
xvi

http://usaisr.amedd.army.mil/pdfs/TCCC_Guidelines_140602.pdf
xvii http://www.hemcon.com/Default.aspx?tabid=489
xviii http://www.israelifirstaid.com/4-israeli-bandage-with-pressure-bar/
xix Butler, Frank. "Management of Open Pneumothorax in Tactical Combat Casualty Care: TCC Guidelines Change 13-02." Journal of Special Operations Medicine Volume 13, Edition 3/Fall 2013
xx

http://www.trauma.org/archive/thoracic/CHESTtension.html
xxi

https://www.narescue.com/portal.aspx?CN=B3327DB2521D&BC=D3BB7B9B52AD

Made in the USA
Middletown, DE
05 July 2015